Happy Holidays!

Diwali

by Rebecca Sabelko

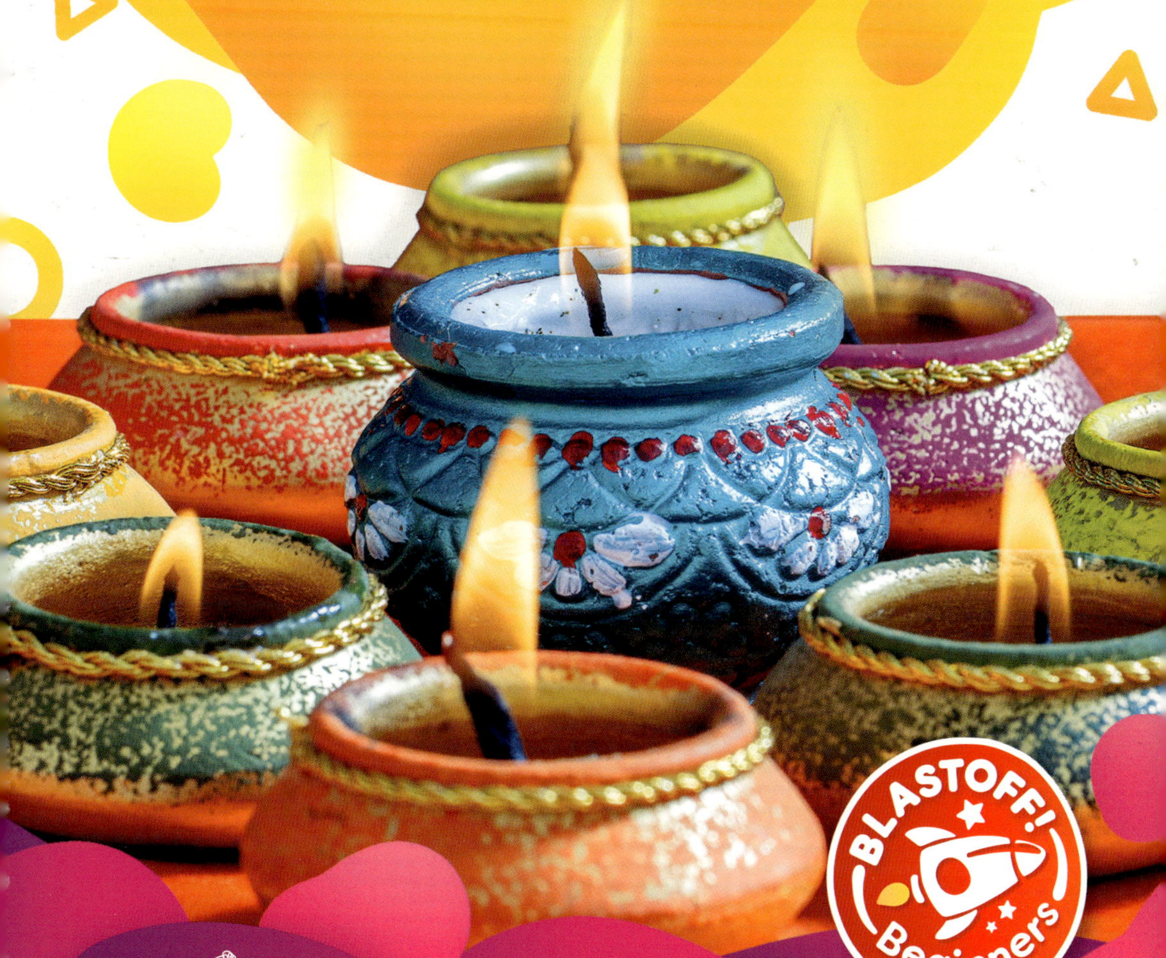

BLASTOFF! Beginners

BELLWETHER MEDIA
MINNEAPOLIS, MN

Blastoff! Beginners are developed by literacy experts and educators to meet the needs of early readers. These engaging informational texts support young children as they begin reading about their world. Through simple language and high frequency words paired with crisp, colorful photos, Blastoff! Beginners launch young readers into the universe of independent reading.

Sight Words in This Book

a	each	is	other	they
are	eat	it	part	time
big	for	make	people	too
called	good	of	the	use
day	in	on	their	

This edition first published in 2023 by Bellwether Media, Inc.

No part of this publication may be reproduced in whole or in part without written permission of the publisher. For information regarding permission, write to Bellwether Media, Inc., Attention: Permissions Department, 6012 Blue Circle Drive, Minnetonka, MN 55343.

Library of Congress Cataloging-in-Publication Data

LC record for Diwali available at: https://lccn.loc.gov/2022009278

Text copyright © 2023 by Bellwether Media, Inc. BLASTOFF! BEGINNERS and associated logos are trademarks and/or registered trademarks of Bellwether Media, Inc.

Editor: Christina Leaf   Designer: Laura Sowers

Printed in the United States of America, North Mankato, MN.

Table of Contents

It Is Diwali!	4
Five Special Days!	6
A Time for Good	12
Diwali Facts	22
Glossary	23
To Learn More	24
Index	24

It Is Diwali!

Happy Diwali! Time for the **Festival** of Lights!

Five Special Days!

Diwali honors good winning over bad.

It is a **Hindu** holiday. Other groups honor it, too.

It is in October or November.
It lasts five days.

A Time for Good

People clean their homes. They **pray** each day.

Families light clay lamps. They are called *diyas*.

diya

People make art on floors. They use colored sand.

floor art

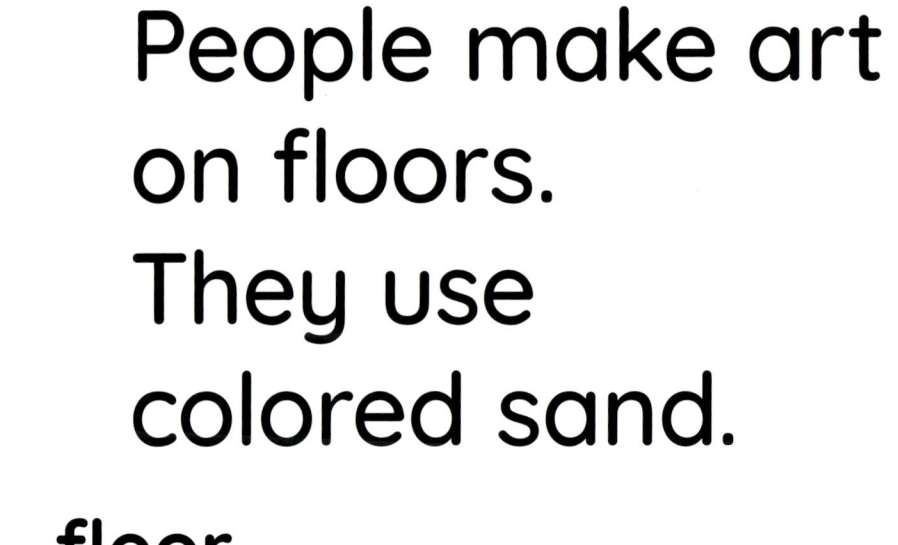

Families eat big meals. Sweets are a favorite part.

sweets

People give gifts. It is a time for good!

gifts

Diwali Facts

Celebrating Diwali

diyas • sweets • gift

Diwali Activities

clean

light diyas

make floor art

Glossary

festival

a joyful event or holiday

Hindu

related to a religion called Hinduism

pray

to speak with or give thanks to a god or gods

To Learn More

ON THE WEB

FACTSURFER

Factsurfer.com gives you a safe, fun way to find more information.

1. Go to www.factsurfer.com.

2. Enter "Diwali" into the search box and click 🔍.

3. Select your book cover to see a list of related content.

Index

art, 16	good, 6, 20	sweets, 18
clean, 12	groups, 8	
days, 10	Hindu, 8	
diyas, 14	homes, 12	
families, 14, 18	meals, 18	
Festival of Lights, 4	November, 10	
	October, 10	
floors, 16	pray, 12, 13	
gifts, 20	sand, 16	

The images in this book are reproduced through the courtesy of: Ami Parikh, front cover; Creative Minds2, p. 3; subodhsathe, pp. 4-5; shibithsnair, pp. 6-7; GCShutter, pp. 8-9; SoumenNath, pp. 10-11; FatCamera, pp. 12-13; deepak bishnoi, p. 14; NIDHI, pp. 14-15, 22 (floor art); StockImageFactory.com, pp. 16, 20; Indiapicture/ Alamy, pp. 16-17; V.S.Anandhakrishna, p. 18; Mila Supinskaya Glashchenko, pp. 18-19; triloks, pp. 20-21; Anant Jadhav, p. 22; SasinTipchai, p. 22 (clean); Reliance CCS, p. 23 (festival); Deepak Sethi, p. 23 (Hindu); Prasannapix, p. 23 (pray).